MW01594777

Breaking The Chain: Empowering Strategies to Deal with a Narcissist

By: Tamara Wood

Copyright © 2023 by Tamara Wood
All rights reserved. This book or any portion
thereof
may not be reproduced or used in any
manner whatsoever
without the express written permission of
the publisher
except for the use of brief quotations in a
book review.

Dedication

To my readers,

You are strong. You are powerful. You are worthy.
You are loved.

You are enough.

Title: Breaking The Chain: Empowering Strategies to Deal with a Narcissist

Table of Contents:

Note: Dealing with a narcissist can be a complex and challenging experience. This book aims to provide guidance, support, and practical strategies to help individuals cope with and overcome the effects of narcissistic relationships. It is essential to prioritize your safety and well-being throughout the process. Remember, you are not alone, and there is hope for a brighter future beyond the grasp of a narcissist.

Introduction: Understanding Narcissism and Its Impact

Welcome to "Breaking The Chain: Empowering Strategies to Deal with a Narcissist." In this book, we embark on a journey of understanding narcissism and equipping ourselves with the knowledge and tools necessary to navigate the challenges it presents. Whether you have personally experienced a relationship with a narcissist or are seeking to support someone who has, this book aims to provide you with valuable insights and practical strategies to regain control, rebuild your life, and foster healthy relationships.

Narcissism, rooted in Greek mythology, takes its name from Narcissus, a young man who fell in love with his own reflection. Similarly, individuals with narcissistic personality disorder (NPD) display an inflated sense of self-importance, an insatiable need for admiration, and a lack of empathy for others. While it is normal for people to have some degree of self-focus, narcissism becomes problematic when it significantly impairs one's ability to form healthy relationships and function in society.

The impact of narcissism on those in close proximity to narcissistic individuals can be devastating. Emotional abuse, manipulation, gaslighting, and constant criticism are just a few of the tactics narcissists employ to maintain their control and power. As a result, victims often experience low self-esteem, anxiety, depression, and a distorted perception of reality.

This book aims to shed light on the dynamics of narcissistic relationships, helping you recognize the traits and patterns that define narcissistic behavior. Armed with this understanding, you can reclaim your power, protect your well-being, and break free from the toxic grip of a narcissist.

Throughout the chapters, we will explore practical strategies to empower yourself in the face of narcissism. From establishing healthy boundaries and practicing self-care to detaching emotionally and seeking professional support, each step is designed to help you regain your sense of self and rebuild a fulfilling life.

It is crucial to note that dealing with a narcissist can be a complex and emotionally challenging process. However, remember that you are not alone. By sharing experiences, insights, and tools, this book aims to provide you with the support and encouragement you need to overcome the adversity and emerge stronger on the other side.

As we delve into the pages ahead, keep an open mind, be patient with yourself, and recognize that healing is a journey. Together, let us embark on this path toward freedom, empowerment, and a life free from the clutches of a narcissist.

This book is designed to help individuals navigate the intricate and often tumultuous terrain of dealing with a narcissist. Whether you are in a relationship with a narcissistic partner, have a narcissistic family member, or encounter narcissistic individuals in other areas of your life, this book aims to equip you with the knowledge and tools needed to protect yourself and regain control of your life.

Narcissism is a personality disorder characterized by an exaggerated sense of self-importance, a constant need for admiration and validation, and a lack of empathy for others. While everyone possesses some narcissistic traits to varying degrees, it is when these traits become pervasive and destructive that they can have a profound impact on relationships and overall well-being.

Living or interacting with a narcissist can be an emotionally draining experience. Their manipulative tactics, emotional abuse, and relentless pursuit of self-interest can leave you feeling diminished, invalidated, and trapped. It is crucial to recognize the signs and patterns of narcissistic behavior in order to protect yourself and establish healthy boundaries.

In this book, we will delve into the intricate details of narcissism, exploring the different types of narcissists, the red flags to watch out for, and the insidious nature of the narcissistic cycle. By understanding the underlying mechanisms of narcissism, you will be better equipped to recognize and respond to their tactics effectively.

Furthermore, we will explore the emotional landscape that accompanies interactions with a narcissist. Gaslighting, a common manipulation technique employed by narcissists, can distort your sense of reality and self-worth. We will discuss strategies for combating gaslighting and regaining your confidence.

Empowerment is a central theme throughout this book. We will guide you in building inner strength, setting boundaries, and practicing assertiveness. By prioritizing self-care and nurturing your emotional well-being, you will be better equipped to navigate the challenges posed by a narcissist.

Detaching from a narcissist can be a challenging yet vital step in reclaiming your life. We will provide practical strategies such as implementing the no-contact rule, utilizing the gray rock technique, and building a support system. Additionally, we will address legal considerations and offer guidance for co-parenting with a narcissistic partner.

Healing and thriving after dealing with a narcissist is a transformative journey. We will explore the post-narcissistic recovery process, focusing on self-reflection, personal growth, and resilience-building. You will learn to rebuild your life and cultivate healthy relationships based on trust and authenticity.

Remember, you are not alone in this journey. Countless individuals have faced similar challenges and have emerged stronger on the other side. This book is here to provide you with the knowledge, support, and strategies necessary to break free from the grip of a narcissist and reclaim your power and happiness.

Now, let us embark on this empowering journey together and learn how to navigate the complexities of dealing with a narcissist.

Chapter 1: Unmasking Narcissism: Identifying the Traits and Patterns

In this chapter, we will dive into the world of narcissism and explore the traits and patterns that define this personality disorder. Understanding these characteristics is crucial in identifying and dealing with narcissistic individuals effectively. By unmasking narcissism, you will gain valuable insights into their behavior and motivations.

1.1 The Narcissistic Personality: An Overview

- Definition of narcissism as a personality disorder

- The origins and development of narcissistic traits

- Common misconceptions and myths about narcissism

- The distinction between healthy self-esteem and pathological narcissism

1.2 Types of Narcissists: Recognizing the Subtle Differences

- Grandiose narcissists: Their inflated sense of self and need for admiration.

- Vulnerable narcissists: The paradoxical combination of self-centeredness and insecurity

- Covert narcissists: The hidden manipulators who operate in subtle ways.

- Malignant narcissists: The most toxic and dangerous form of narcissism

1.3 Red Flags: Warning Signs of Narcissistic Behavior

- Excessive self-importance and a sense of entitlement

- Lack of empathy and disregard for others' feelings

- Constant need for admiration and validation

- Manipulative behaviors and emotional exploitation

- Fragile self-esteem and a tendency to react aggressively to criticism.

1.4 The Narcissistic Cycle: Understanding Their Manipulative Tactics

- Idealization: The charm offensive and love bombing stage

- Devaluation: The sudden shift to criticism, belittlement, and devaluation

- Discard: The ultimate rejection and withdrawal of attention and affection

- Hoovering: The cycle of reeling you back in after a discard

- Rinse and repeat: The repetitive nature of the narcissistic cycle

By the end of this chapter, you will have a clear understanding of the various types of narcissists and the red flags that indicate their presence. Armed with this knowledge, you will be better prepared to recognize narcissistic behavior in your relationships and interactions. Remember, identifying the traits and patterns of narcissism is the first step towards dealing with it effectively and protecting your emotional well-being.

1.1 The Narcissistic Personality: An Overview

Narcissism, as a personality disorder, is characterized by a pervasive pattern of grandiosity, a constant need for admiration, and a lack of empathy for others. Individuals with narcissistic personality disorder (NPD) have an inflated sense of self-importance, believe they are special and unique, and require excessive admiration and attention from others to maintain their fragile self-esteem.

The origins and development of narcissistic traits can be influenced by a variety of factors. Childhood experiences, such as excessive praise or neglect, inconsistent parenting styles, or trauma, may contribute to the development of narcissistic tendencies. Some experts also suggest that genetic and neurobiological factors may play a role in the manifestation of narcissistic personality traits.

It is essential to debunk common misconceptions and myths about narcissism to gain a more accurate understanding of this complex disorder. One common misconception is that all individuals who exhibit narcissistic traits are full-blown narcissists. In reality, narcissism exists on a spectrum, and some people may display narcissistic traits without meeting the criteria for NPD. Another myth is that all narcissists are overtly arrogant and boastful. While grandiose narcissists often exhibit these traits, other types of narcissists may hide their self-centeredness behind a more reserved and subtle demeanor.

Distinguishing between healthy self-esteem and pathological narcissism is crucial for understanding the impact of narcissistic behavior. Healthy self-esteem involves having a balanced and realistic view of oneself, with an appreciation for one's strengths and acceptance of limitations. Pathological narcissism, on the other hand, is characterized by an inflated and unrealistic sense of self, a constant need for validation, and a disregard for others' feelings and boundaries. The key distinction lies in the narcissist's inability to form genuine connections and their manipulative and exploitative behaviors.

Recognizing the difference between healthy self-esteem and pathological narcissism allows us to approach narcissistic individuals with empathy and understanding, while also maintaining boundaries to protect ourselves from potential harm.

In conclusion, understanding the narcissistic personality is essential in dealing with narcissistic individuals. By recognizing narcissism as a personality disorder, understanding its origins, debunking misconceptions, and distinguishing between healthy self-esteem and pathological narcissism, we can develop a clearer perspective on this complex phenomenon. This knowledge forms the foundation for effectively navigating relationships with narcissistic individuals and protecting our own well-being.

1.2 Types of Narcissists: Recognizing the Subtle Differences

Narcissism is not a one-size-fits-all personality disorder. There are different types of narcissists, each exhibiting unique characteristics and behaviors. By understanding these distinctions, you can better identify and navigate relationships with narcissistic individuals. Here are four common types of narcissists:

1. Grandiose Narcissists: Grandiose narcissists are often what comes to mind when we think of narcissism. They have an exaggerated sense of self-importance and believe they are superior to others. They crave constant admiration and attention, seeking validation to maintain their fragile self-esteem. Grandiose narcissists may display overt arrogance, boastfulness, and a sense of entitlement. They are often charismatic and may use charm to manipulate others.

2. Vulnerable Narcissists: Vulnerable narcissists demonstrate a paradoxical combination of self-centeredness and deep insecurity. They may appear shy or introverted, but they still crave attention and admiration. Unlike grandiose narcissists, who overtly project

superiority, vulnerable narcissists may portray themselves as victims or martyr-like figures. They constantly seek reassurance, validation, and empathy from others, often using their perceived fragility to manipulate and control situations.

3. Covert Narcissists: Covert narcissists operate in a more hidden and subtle manner compared to their grandiose counterparts. They may present themselves as selfless, empathetic individuals, while covertly seeking power, control, and admiration behind the scenes. Covert narcissists often use passive-aggressive tactics, manipulation, and playing the victim to achieve their desired outcomes. They excel at gaining sympathy and evoking guilt in others to maintain control over relationships.

4. Malignant Narcissists: Malignant narcissists represent the most dangerous and toxic form of narcissism. They combine the traits of grandiosity, lack of empathy, and a willingness to exploit others for their own gain. Malignant narcissists exhibit a pattern of sadistic behavior, showing pleasure in inflicting harm on others. They may engage in gaslighting, manipulation, and even aggressive or abusive actions. These individuals pose a significant threat to the well-being and safety of those around them.

It's important to note that individuals with narcissistic traits can exhibit a combination of these types, making it challenging to categorize them solely into one category. Additionally, the severity of narcissistic traits can vary among individuals.

Understanding the different types of narcissists can help you recognize their behaviors and motivations. It enables you to develop effective strategies for setting boundaries, managing interactions, and protecting yourself from their manipulative tactics. Remember, dealing with narcissists requires careful observation and self-care, as their behaviors can be emotionally draining and damaging.

1.3 Red Flags: Warning Signs of Narcissistic Behavior

Recognizing the red flags and warning signs of narcissistic behavior is crucial in identifying and dealing with narcissistic individuals. While not all narcissists exhibit every sign, these common indicators can help you assess the presence of narcissistic traits in someone's behavior:

1. Excessive self-importance and a sense of entitlement: Narcissists often have an inflated sense of their own importance and believe they are special or superior to others. They may exhibit a constant need for

attention, admiration, and recognition, expecting special treatment and privileges.

2. Lack of empathy and disregard for others' feelings: One of the defining characteristics of narcissism is a lack of empathy. Narcissists struggle to understand or care about others' emotions, needs, or perspectives. They prioritize their own desires and goals over the well-being of others, leading to a pattern of disregard for others' feelings and boundaries.

3. Constant need for admiration and validation: Narcissists crave constant attention, praise, and validation from others to maintain their fragile self-esteem. They seek admiration and may fish for compliments or engage in self-promotion to feed their ego. They are often preoccupied with their image and external validation.

4. Manipulative behaviors and emotional exploitation: Narcissists are skilled manipulators who employ various tactics to control and exploit others. They may use charm, flattery, or charisma to gain trust and influence. Additionally, they are adept at gaslighting, distorting reality, and undermining your confidence, leaving you confused and doubting your own perceptions.

5. Fragile self-esteem and a tendency to react aggressively to criticism: Despite their grandiose facade, narcissists have fragile self-esteem. They are highly sensitive to criticism and rejection, often responding with defensiveness, anger, or aggression. They may lash out, belittle, or devalue those who challenge their sense of superiority.

These red flags serve as important indicators for identifying narcissistic behavior. However, it is essential to consider patterns of behavior rather than isolated incidents. A single sign does not definitively label someone as a narcissist, but if you observe a consistent presence of these red flags in someone's behavior, it may suggest the presence of narcissistic traits.

By recognizing these warning signs, you can better protect yourself, set boundaries, and make informed decisions about your interactions with narcissistic individuals. Remember, your well-being is paramount, and understanding these red flags empowers you to navigate relationships with greater awareness and self-care.

1.4 The Narcissistic Cycle: Understanding Their Manipulative Tactics

Dealing with a narcissist often involves navigating a predictable cycle of behaviors known as the narcissistic cycle. Understanding this cycle can help you recognize their manipulative tactics and protect yourself from the emotional roller coaster it entails. Here are the stages of the narcissistic cycle:

1. Idealization: During the idealization stage, the narcissist puts on a charm offensive, showering you with attention, affection, and compliments. They may engage in love bombing, overwhelming you with affection and making you feel like the center of their world. This stage is designed to create an intense bond and gain your trust and admiration.

2. Devaluation: Once the idealization stage fades, the narcissist's true colors start to emerge. They may abruptly shift from adoration to criticism, belittlement, and devaluation. The devaluation stage involves undermining your self-esteem, pointing out your flaws, and making you feel unworthy or inadequate. This is a tactic used to maintain control and power over you.

3. Discard: At some point, the narcissist may discard you. This can happen suddenly and without warning. They withdraw their attention, affection, and validation, leaving you feeling confused, rejected, and abandoned. The discard stage is meant to exert further control by instilling fear and dependence.

4. Hoovering: After the discard, the narcissist may attempt to reel you back into the relationship. They may use manipulation tactics, such as guilt-tripping, promises of change, or creating a sense of urgency, to regain control and attention. The hoovering stage aims to reignite the hope and attachment you had for them.

5. Rinse and repeat: The narcissistic cycle is not a one-time occurrence; it often repeats itself in a continuous loop. The idealization, devaluation, discard, and hoovering stages can cycle through repeatedly, creating a pattern of emotional highs and lows. This cycle serves to keep you emotionally invested, dependent, and under the narcissist's control.

Understanding the narcissistic cycle allows you to recognize the manipulative tactics employed by narcissists. By being aware of these stages, you can protect yourself from falling into their traps and establish healthy boundaries. It is important to note that breaking free from this cycle often requires distancing yourself from the narcissist and seeking support from trusted individuals or professionals.

Remember, the narcissistic cycle is a manipulative pattern that seeks to exploit and control you. By recognizing the stages and dynamics involved, you can empower yourself to break free and regain control over your own emotional well-being.

Chapter 2: The Emotional Landscape: Navigating the Effects of Narcissism

Dealing with a narcissist can take a toll on your emotional well-being. In this chapter, we will explore the emotional landscape that accompanies interactions with narcissistic individuals. Understanding these effects is essential in developing strategies to protect yourself and heal from the impact of narcissism.

2.1 Emotional Manipulation: Gaslighting and Mind Games

- Gaslighting: The tactic of distorting reality and making you doubt your perceptions.

- Mind games: Psychological tactics used to confuse, control, and manipulate.

- The effects of emotional manipulation on your self-esteem and confidence

2.2 Self-Doubt and Second-Guessing: Rebuilding Trust in Yourself

- The constant questioning of your thoughts, feelings, and judgments

- Rebuilding self-trust and regaining confidence in your own perceptions

- Recognizing your strengths and affirming your worth

2.3 Emotional Exhaustion and Burnout: Prioritizing Self-Care

- The draining nature of interactions with narcissists

- Setting boundaries and practicing self-care to prevent emotional exhaustion.

- Seeking support systems and professional help to cope with burnout.

2.4 Healing from Emotional Trauma: Recovery and Empowerment

- Recognizing the emotional trauma caused by narcissistic abuse.

- Processing and healing from the effects of the abuse

- Reclaiming your power, rebuilding your self-esteem, and moving forward

2.5 Establishing Healthy Boundaries: Protecting Your Emotional Well-being

- The importance of setting clear and firm boundaries with narcissistic individuals

- Strategies for assertiveness and boundary enforcement

- Detaching emotionally and reducing contact with toxic individuals

Navigating the emotional landscape of dealing with a narcissist can be challenging, but it is essential for your own healing and growth. By understanding the tactics of emotional manipulation, rebuilding trust in yourself, prioritizing self-care, healing from emotional trauma, and establishing healthy boundaries, you can regain control over your emotions and protect your well-being.

Throughout this chapter, we will provide practical tips, exercises, and guidance to help you navigate these emotional challenges and move toward a healthier and more empowered state of being. Remember, healing from the effects of narcissism is a journey, and with the right tools and support, you can reclaim your emotional well-being and thrive.

2.1 Emotional Abuse: Recognizing the Damage

Interactions with narcissistic individuals often involve emotional abuse, which can have long-lasting effects on your well-being. In this section, we will explore the various ways emotional abuse manifests and how it impacts your emotional state.

1. Gaslighting: Gaslighting is a manipulative tactic used by narcissists to distort your reality and make you doubt your own perceptions, memories, and sanity. They may deny events or conversations, manipulate facts, or make you feel like you're overreacting or being overly sensitive. Gaslighting erodes your self-trust and can leave you confused and questioning your own sanity.

2. Verbal and Emotional Attacks: Narcissists may engage in constant criticism, insults, belittlement, or humiliation. They may undermine your self-esteem, attack your character, and make derogatory remarks about your abilities, appearance, or intelligence. These verbal and emotional attacks can chip away at your self-worth, leaving you feeling worthless, powerless, and emotionally drained.

3. Manipulation and Control: Narcissists excel at manipulation tactics to gain control over you. They may use guilt, manipulation, and emotional blackmail to get what they want. They exploit your vulnerabilities, fears, and desires to manipulate your actions and emotions. The constant manipulation leaves you feeling trapped, controlled, and unable to assert your own needs and desires.

4. Isolation and Alienation: Narcissists often isolate their victims from friends, family, and support networks. They may portray themselves as the only ones who truly understand and care for you, while maligning and criticizing others in your life. This isolation leaves you dependent on the narcissist for validation, support, and companionship, further enhancing their control over you.

5. Emotional Roller Coaster: Interacting with a narcissist can feel like a constant roller coaster ride. They create an unpredictable and chaotic environment, oscillating between idealization and devaluation. The inconsistency and instability can leave you anxious, on edge, and always trying to please the narcissist to avoid their wrath.

The damage caused by emotional abuse is significant and can impact your self-esteem, confidence, and overall emotional well-being. It is crucial to recognize these signs of emotional abuse and acknowledge the toll it takes on you. Understanding the nature of emotional abuse empowers you to break free from its grip and begin the journey toward healing and recovery.

In the next sections, we will delve into strategies for rebuilding your self-esteem, setting boundaries, and finding support systems to assist you in your healing process. Remember, you deserve to be treated with respect, kindness, and empathy, and by recognizing the damage of emotional abuse, you can take the first steps towards reclaiming your emotional well-being.

2.2 Gaslighting: Challenging Your Reality

Gaslighting is a manipulative tactic employed by narcissists to undermine your perceptions, memories, and sense of reality. It can leave you feeling confused, doubting your own sanity, and dependent on the narcissist for validation. In this section, we will explore strategies to challenge gaslighting and regain trust in your own reality.

1. Recognize the Signs: Educate yourself about gaslighting and become familiar with its signs. Pay attention to instances where the narcissist denies or twists facts, contradicts their previous statements, or dismisses your concerns and feelings. Recognizing the

patterns of gaslighting is the first step in combating its effects.

2. Validate Your Experiences: Trust your own experiences and emotions. Gaslighting aims to make you doubt yourself, but you have a right to your feelings and perceptions. Remind yourself that your experiences are valid and deserving of consideration. Seek validation from trusted friends, family, or professionals who can provide an objective perspective and support your reality.

3. Document Incidents: Keep a record of gaslighting incidents, including dates, times, and specific examples. This documentation serves as a tangible reminder of the gaslighting tactics used against you. It can help you maintain clarity and combat the narcissist's attempts to rewrite history. Reviewing this evidence can reinforce your trust in your own experiences.

4. Seek External Validation: Reach out to trusted individuals who can provide validation and support. Share your experiences with them and seek their perspective. Discussing your concerns with someone who understands and believes you can help validate your reality and counteract the gaslighting. Their support can provide you with the strength to challenge the narcissist's manipulation.

5. Establish Boundaries: Set clear boundaries with the narcissist regarding what behavior is acceptable and what is not. Communicate your needs and expectations assertively and confidently. By setting boundaries, you assert your autonomy and protect yourself from further gaslighting. Be prepared for the narcissist to challenge your boundaries, but remain firm in upholding them.

6. Trust Your Intuition: Listen to your gut instincts. Your intuition is a powerful tool that can guide you in recognizing manipulation and deception. If something feels off or contradictory, trust yourself. Tune into your instincts and honor your inner voice. Cultivating self-trust is essential in countering gaslighting and reclaiming your sense of reality.

7. Seek Professional Support: Consider seeking support from a therapist or counselor experienced in dealing with narcissistic abuse. They can provide guidance, validation, and techniques to help you navigate the effects of gaslighting. Therapy can provide a safe space to process your experiences, regain confidence, and develop coping strategies.

Challenging gaslighting takes time and self-compassion. It requires reestablishing trust in your own perceptions and experiences. By recognizing the signs, seeking external validation, documenting incidents, setting boundaries, trusting your intuition, and seeking professional support, you can break free from the grip of gaslighting and regain a solid foundation of self-trust. Remember, you are not alone, and your reality matters.

2.3 Walking on Eggshells: Coping with Constant Tension

Interacting with a narcissist often involves walking on eggshells to avoid triggering their anger, criticism, or manipulation. This constant tension can be emotionally exhausting and impact your well-being. In this section, we will explore strategies to cope with the ongoing stress and create a healthier environment for yourself.

1. Recognize the Patterns: Become aware of the triggers and patterns that lead to tense interactions with the narcissist. Pay attention to their behavior, your responses, and the resulting consequences. Understanding these patterns can help you anticipate and navigate challenging situations more effectively.

2. Self-Reflection and Emotional Regulation: Take time for self-reflection and emotional regulation. Prioritize your own emotional well-being by engaging in activities that help you relax, de-stress, and process your emotions. Practice deep breathing, meditation, journaling, or engaging in hobbies that bring you joy. Developing emotional resilience and self-awareness can help you navigate tense interactions more calmly.

3. Set Clear Boundaries: Establish clear boundaries with the narcissist to protect your emotional well-being. Communicate your limits and expectations assertively and be consistent in enforcing them. Setting boundaries sends a message that you will not tolerate abusive or manipulative behavior, and it helps you regain a sense of control in your interactions.

4. Seek Support: Build a strong support network of trusted friends, family, or support groups who understand your situation and can provide emotional support. Share your experiences and feelings with them, seek their guidance, and lean on them during challenging times. Having a supportive community can provide validation, comfort, and perspective.

5. Develop Coping Strategies: Identify healthy coping strategies that work for you. Engage in activities that help you relax and recharge, such as exercise, spending time in nature, practicing mindfulness, or pursuing creative outlets. Developing a toolbox of coping strategies allows you to proactively manage stress and maintain your emotional well-being.

6. Practice Self-Compassion: Be gentle with yourself and practice self-compassion. Recognize that dealing with a narcissist is

challenging, and it is not your fault. Acknowledge your efforts and progress, even if they seem small. Treat yourself with kindness, understanding, and patience as you navigate the difficult dynamics.

7. Professional Guidance: Consider seeking professional guidance from therapists or counselors experienced in narcissistic abuse. They can provide additional tools, techniques, and support tailored to your specific situation. A professional can help you process your emotions, develop coping strategies, and navigate the complexities of dealing with a narcissist.

Remember, your well-being is a priority. Coping with constant tension requires self-care, boundaries, support, and self-compassion. By implementing these strategies, you can regain a sense of control, reduce the emotional toll, and create a healthier space for yourself amidst the challenging dynamics with a narcissist.

2.4 Cognitive Dissonance: Reconciling the Conflicting Realities

Dealing with a narcissist often involves experiencing cognitive dissonance, a state of internal conflict caused by holding contradictory beliefs or perceptions. The narcissist's manipulative tactics and inconsistent behaviors can create a stark contrast between the charming facade they present and the abusive or manipulative behaviors they exhibit. In this section, we will explore strategies to navigate cognitive dissonance and find clarity amidst the conflicting realities.

1. Validate Your Feelings: Acknowledge and validate the conflicting emotions you experience. It is natural to feel confused, frustrated, or torn when faced with contradictory behaviors from the narcissist. Recognize that your emotional responses are valid and deserve to be acknowledged.

2. Seek External Perspective: Reach out to trusted individuals outside the situation who can provide an objective perspective. Share your experiences with them and listen to their insights. Sometimes, an outsider's viewpoint can help shed light on the dynamics and assist in reconciling the conflicting realities.

3. Educate Yourself: Learn more about narcissism and the manipulation tactics commonly employed by narcissists. Understanding the patterns and behaviors associated with narcissistic personality disorder can help you make sense of the contradictions you observe. Educating yourself empowers you to navigate the situation with greater clarity.

4. Trust Your Observations: Reaffirm your trust in your own observations and experiences. Remind yourself that you have witnessed both the positive and negative aspects of the narcissist's behavior. Trust your intuition and pay attention to the red flags and warning signs you have observed. Trusting yourself is crucial in reconciling conflicting realities.

5. Document Incidents: Keep a journal or record of specific incidents that highlight the contradictory behaviors of the narcissist. Writing down these instances can help you gain clarity and prevent the narcissist from gaslighting or distorting the truth. Refer to your documentation as a reminder of the inconsistencies you have witnessed.

6. Focus on Patterns, Not Moments: Instead of getting caught up in isolated moments of positive or negative interactions, look for consistent patterns of behavior. Reflect on the long-term behavior patterns of the narcissist and the impact they have had on your emotional well-being. This broader perspective can help you reconcile the conflicting realities.

7. Practice Self-Reflection: Engage in self-reflection to gain insight into your own values, boundaries, and needs. Clarify what you truly want and deserve in your relationships. Self-reflection allows you to

align your actions and decisions with your authentic self, helping you navigate the conflicting realities with more clarity and conviction.

8. Establish Boundaries: Setting and enforcing clear boundaries is essential when dealing with conflicting realities. Define what behaviors you will tolerate and what you will not. Communicate these boundaries assertively to the narcissist and reinforce them consistently. Boundaries provide a framework for navigating the complexities of the relationship.

9. Seek Professional Support: Consider seeking professional support from therapists or counselors who specialize in narcissistic abuse. They can provide guidance, validation, and strategies to help you navigate cognitive dissonance and reconcile the conflicting realities. A professional can offer insights and tools to support your emotional well-being throughout the process.

Reconciling conflicting realities requires self-trust, external perspectives, education, and self-reflection. By validating your feelings, seeking outside support, educating yourself, trusting your observations, documenting incidents, focusing on patterns, practicing self-reflection, establishing boundaries, and seeking professional guidance, you can navigate the cognitive dissonance and find greater clarity in your interactions with a narcissist. Remember, you have the power to define your reality and make choices that align with your well-being.

Chapter 3: Empowering Yourself: Building Inner Strength and Boundaries

Dealing with a narcissist can be draining and challenging, but it is crucial to empower yourself and build inner strength and boundaries to protect your well-being. In this chapter, we will explore various strategies and practices to help you reclaim your power, establish healthy boundaries, and foster your personal growth.

3.1 Understanding Your Worth: Cultivating Self-Esteem

1. Self-Reflection: Engage in self-reflection to gain a deeper understanding of your values, strengths, and unique qualities. Recognize and appreciate your worth beyond the opinions and validation of the narcissist. Celebrate your achievements, talents, and the positive impact you have on others.

2. Self-Care: Prioritize self-care activities that nurture your physical, emotional, and mental well-being. Engage in activities that bring you joy, relaxation, and fulfillment. Set aside time for rest, exercise, healthy eating, hobbies,

and spending time with loved ones. Self-care reinforces your sense of self-worth and helps you recharge.

3. Affirmations: Practice positive affirmations to counteract the negative self-talk that may have been instilled by the narcissist. Repeat affirmations that highlight your strengths, resilience, and inherent worthiness. Internalize these affirmations to build a strong foundation of self-esteem.

4. Surround Yourself with Supportive People: Surround yourself with individuals who uplift and support you. Cultivate relationships with people who value and appreciate you for who you are. Seek out supportive friends, family members, or support groups where you can share your experiences and receive encouragement.

3.2 Establishing Healthy Boundaries

1. Identify Your Boundaries: Reflect on your values, needs, and limits. Identify the boundaries you want to establish in your interactions with the narcissist. Determine what behaviors are unacceptable and communicate these boundaries clearly.

2. Communicate Assertively: Practice assertive communication to express your boundaries effectively. Clearly and confidently articulate

your needs, expectations, and limits to the narcissist. Use "I" statements to convey your feelings and assert your boundaries without aggression or hostility.

3. Enforce Boundaries: Be consistent in enforcing your boundaries. Do not waver or compromise your boundaries for the sake of appeasing the narcissist. Clearly communicate the consequences of crossing your boundaries and follow through with appropriate actions if they are violated.

4. Self-Validation: Validate and trust your own feelings and perceptions. Do not rely solely on external validation from the narcissist. Remember that you have the right to your emotions and experiences, regardless of how the narcissist may try to invalidate them.

5. Practice Self-Care: Engage in self-care practices that support your emotional well-being. Prioritize activities that promote self-reflection, relaxation, and personal growth. Taking care of yourself strengthens your ability to maintain boundaries and navigate challenging interactions.

3.3 Building Resilience and Coping Strategies

1. Develop Emotional Resilience: Cultivate emotional resilience by practicing self-compassion, developing healthy coping

mechanisms, and seeking support from trusted individuals. Focus on building your capacity to bounce back from adversity and remain emotionally strong.

2. Set Realistic Expectations: Adjust your expectations of the narcissist's behavior and accept that you cannot change or control them. Instead, focus on managing your own reactions and choices. By setting realistic expectations, you reduce the potential for disappointment and frustration.

3. Seek Professional Help: Consider seeking professional help from therapists or counselors specializing in narcissistic abuse. They can provide valuable guidance, support, and tools to help you navigate the challenges and heal from the effects of the relationship.

4. Practice Mindfulness: Engage in mindfulness practices to cultivate self-awareness, presence, and inner calm. Mindfulness allows you to observe your thoughts and emotions without judgment, empowering you to respond rather than react to the narcissist's manipulations.

5. Build a Supportive Network: Surround yourself with a supportive network of individuals who understand your experiences and offer unconditional support. Seek out support groups or online communities where

you can connect with others who have faced similar challenges.

By cultivating self-esteem, establishing healthy boundaries, and building resilience, you can empower yourself in dealing with a narcissist. Remember, your well-being is a priority, and you have the strength within you to navigate these difficult dynamics.

3.1 Understanding Your Worth: Reclaiming Your Self-Esteem

Dealing with a narcissist can often erode your self-esteem and make you question your worth. In this section, we will explore strategies to help you understand and reclaim your self-esteem, allowing you to rebuild your sense of self-worth and confidence.

1. Self-Reflection and Self-Acceptance: Engage in self-reflection to gain a deeper understanding of yourself. Identify your values, strengths, and accomplishments. Reflect on your unique qualities and what makes you special. Practice self-acceptance by embracing both your strengths and areas for growth. Recognize that you are a valuable individual deserving of love and respect.

2. Challenge Negative Self-Talk: Become aware of the negative self-talk that may have been instilled by the narcissist. Challenge those negative thoughts and replace them with positive and empowering affirmations. Remind yourself of your worth, capabilities, and achievements. Focus on your strengths and the positive aspects of your personality and life.

3. Cultivate Self-Care: Prioritize self-care activities that nurture your physical, emotional, and mental well-being. Engage in activities that bring you joy, relaxation, and fulfillment. This can include practicing mindfulness, engaging in hobbies you enjoy, spending time in nature, or engaging in activities that promote self-expression. Taking care of yourself demonstrates self-love and reinforces your self-esteem.

4. Surround Yourself with Supportive People: Surround yourself with individuals who uplift and support you. Seek out relationships with people who appreciate and value you for who you are. Build a support network of friends, family members, or support groups where you can share your experiences, receive validation, and gain perspective. Positive and supportive relationships can bolster your self-esteem.

5. Set and Achieve Realistic Goals: Set realistic goals for yourself and work towards achieving them. Start with small, achievable steps that align with your values and aspirations. As you accomplish these goals, your sense of self-worth and confidence will grow. Celebrate your achievements, no matter how small, and use them as fuel to propel yourself forward.

6.   Practice Self-Compassion: Be compassionate towards yourself as you navigate the challenges of dealing with a narcissist. Acknowledge that it is not your fault and that you are doing the best you can in a difficult situation. Treat yourself with kindness, understanding, and patience. Practice self-compassion by offering yourself the same support and encouragement you would give to a dear friend.

7.   Seek Professional Support: Consider seeking professional support from therapists or counselors who specialize in narcissistic abuse. They can provide guidance, validation, and tools to help you rebuild your self-esteem. A professional can assist you in processing your emotions, challenging negative beliefs, and developing strategies to enhance your self-worth.

Reclaiming your self-esteem is a journey that requires self-reflection, self-care, positive affirmations, supportive relationships, and professional support. Remember, you are deserving of love, respect, and happiness. By nurturing your self-esteem, you can regain your confidence and thrive beyond the impact of the narcissistic relationship.

3.2 Setting Boundaries: Establishing Healthy Limits

When dealing with a narcissist, setting and maintaining boundaries is crucial to protect your well-being and regain a sense of control in the relationship. Establishing healthy limits empowers you to define what is acceptable and what is not, ensuring that your needs and values are respected. Here are some strategies to help you set boundaries effectively:

1. Identify Your Values and Needs: Reflect on your values, needs, and priorities. Understand what is important to you in relationships and what behaviors you find unacceptable. This self-awareness will serve as a foundation for establishing boundaries that align with your values and promote your well-being.

2. Communicate Clearly and Assertively: Clearly communicate your boundaries to the narcissist in a calm and assertive manner. Use "I" statements to express how their behavior affects you and what you need from them. Be direct and specific, avoiding vague or ambiguous language. Remember that you have the right to set boundaries and assert your needs.

3. Reinforce Boundaries Consistently: Consistency is key when it comes to enforcing boundaries. Once you have communicated your boundaries, reinforce them consistently. Do not waver or make exceptions, as this can be exploited by the narcissist. Show them that your boundaries are non-negotiable and that you expect them to be respected.

4. Use Consequences: Clearly communicate the consequences of crossing your boundaries and follow through with them if necessary. Consequences can include limiting contact, ending a conversation, or taking a break from the relationship. By implementing consequences, you establish that your boundaries are serious and will be upheld.

5. Practice Self-Care: Prioritize self-care as a way to support your boundary-setting process. Taking care of your physical, emotional, and mental well-being reinforces your sense of self-worth and strengthens your ability to assert boundaries. Engage in activities that replenish your energy and help you stay grounded.

6. Seek Support: Reach out to a trusted friend, family member, or therapist who can provide guidance and support as you navigate setting boundaries. They can offer an objective perspective and help you stay accountable to

your own needs. Supportive individuals can validate your experiences and empower you to prioritize your boundaries.

7. Stay Firm and Assertive: Narcissists may push back or try to manipulate you into relinquishing your boundaries. Stay firm and assertive in upholding them. Do not let guilt, fear, or intimidation sway you. Remember that your boundaries are essential for your well-being, and you have the right to maintain them.

8. Reevaluate Relationships: Assess the overall impact of the narcissistic relationship on your well-being. If the narcissist consistently disregards your boundaries and shows no respect for your needs, it may be necessary to reevaluate the relationship. Consider whether it is healthy and beneficial for you to continue the connection.

Remember, setting boundaries is an act of self-care and self-respect. It empowers you to create a healthier dynamic and protects your emotional well-being. While the narcissist may resist or challenge your boundaries, stay committed to prioritizing your needs and building relationships that are built on mutual respect.

3.3 Assertiveness Training: Communicating Effectively

When dealing with a narcissist, assertiveness is a valuable skill that can help you communicate your needs, express your boundaries, and maintain your self-respect. Assertiveness allows you to advocate for yourself without being aggressive or passive. Here are some strategies to help you communicate effectively and assertively:

1. Use "I" Statements: When expressing your feelings or needs, use "I" statements instead of blaming or accusing language. For example, say, "I feel hurt when you dismiss my opinions," instead of, "You always ignore me." This approach takes ownership of your emotions and avoids putting the narcissist on the defensive.

2. Be Clear and Direct: Clearly state what you want or need in a specific and concise manner. Avoid being vague or relying on hints that the narcissist may not pick up on. Use assertive phrases like, "I need some alone time right now" or "I would appreciate it if you could listen without interrupting."

3. Maintain Eye Contact and Body Language: Assertiveness is not just about what you say, but also how you convey your message.

Maintain steady eye contact and use confident body language, such as standing or sitting up straight. Avoid crossing your arms or fidgeting, as these can convey defensiveness or insecurity.

4. Practice Active Listening: Active listening involves not only expressing yourself but also showing genuine interest and understanding in what the other person is saying. Repeat back key points or paraphrase to ensure that you accurately understand their perspective. This demonstrates respect and fosters effective communication.

5. Set Boundaries and Reinforce Them: Clearly state your boundaries and expectations to the narcissist. Be firm in asserting what is acceptable and what is not. Reinforce your boundaries consistently by following through with consequences if they are crossed. This shows the narcissist that your boundaries are non-negotiable.

6. Use Calm and Neutral Tone: Keep your tone of voice calm and neutral, even if the narcissist becomes confrontational or tries to provoke a reaction. Avoid escalating the situation by responding with anger or aggression. Maintain your composure and respond assertively without resorting to personal attacks or insults.

7. Practice Empathy: While it may be challenging, try to understand the underlying motivations and insecurities that drive the narcissist's behavior. This doesn't mean condoning or accepting their actions, but it can help you approach the communication with empathy and compassion.

8. Practice Self-Care: Taking care of yourself is essential for effective communication. Prioritize self-care activities that promote your well-being, reduce stress, and enhance your emotional resilience. When you are grounded and balanced, you are better equipped to assertively communicate your needs.

9. Seek Support: If you find it challenging to communicate assertively with the narcissist, seek support from trusted friends, family, or a therapist. They can provide guidance, help you practice assertiveness techniques, and offer encouragement as you navigate challenging interactions.

Remember, assertiveness is a skill that requires practice and patience. It may take time to feel comfortable asserting yourself, especially with a narcissist. Be persistent and kind to yourself throughout the process and celebrate your progress along the way.

3.4 Self-Care Practices: Nurturing Your Emotional Well-being

Dealing with a narcissist can take a toll on your emotional well-being. It is essential to prioritize self-care to nurture your mental and emotional health. Here are some self-care practices that can support you in navigating the challenges of dealing with a narcissist:

1. Establish Healthy Boundaries: Setting and maintaining healthy boundaries is a form of self-care. Clearly define what is acceptable and what is not in your interactions with the narcissist. Honor your boundaries and communicate them assertively. This will help protect your emotional well-being and preserve your sense of self.

2. Practice Mindfulness and Self-Reflection: Engage in mindfulness practices that help you stay present and centered. This can include meditation, deep breathing exercises, or journaling. Take time for self-reflection to understand your emotions, triggers, and needs. Cultivating self-awareness can empower you to make choices that support your emotional well-being.

3. Engage in Activities You Enjoy: Make time for activities that bring you joy and fulfillment. Engage in hobbies, creative pursuits, or physical activities that you find enjoyable. These activities serve as a form of self-expression and provide a respite from the stress of dealing with a narcissist.

4. Seek Emotional Support: Reach out to trusted friends, family members, or support groups who can provide a listening ear and emotional support. Share your experiences, concerns, and feelings with individuals who understand and validate your experiences. Having a support network can be instrumental in coping with the challenges of dealing with a narcissist.

5. Practice Emotional Release Techniques: Find healthy ways to release and process your emotions. This can include journaling, talking to a therapist, practicing deep breathing exercises, or engaging in physical activities like yoga or running. Find what works best for you to release any pent-up emotions and restore emotional balance.

6. Prioritize Self-Compassion: Be kind and compassionate toward yourself. Recognize that dealing with a narcissist can be emotionally draining and challenging. Practice self-compassion by offering yourself understanding, patience, and self-care. Treat

yourself with the same kindness and compassion you would show to a loved one going through a difficult time.

7.   Set Realistic Expectations: Managing expectations is crucial when dealing with a narcissist. Recognize that you cannot change or control their behavior. Focus on what you can control, such as your own reactions, boundaries, and self-care practices. Setting realistic expectations helps alleviate unnecessary stress and disappointment.

8.   Limit Contact: Consider limiting or reducing contact with the narcissist if it is necessary for your well-being. This may involve setting boundaries around communication, minimizing exposure to their manipulations, or creating physical distance if possible. Prioritize your emotional well-being and make choices that support your healing and growth.

9.   Seek Professional Help: If the emotional impact of dealing with a narcissist becomes overwhelming, consider seeking professional help. A therapist experienced in narcissistic abuse can provide guidance, validation, and tools to help you navigate the emotional challenges and heal from the trauma.

Remember that self-care is not selfish but a necessary act of self-preservation. Prioritizing your emotional well-being allows you to build resilience, maintain your sense of self, and navigate the challenges of dealing with a narcissist more effectively.

Chapter 4: Detaching and Breaking Free: Strategies for Liberation

Dealing with a narcissist can be emotionally draining and detrimental to your well-being. In this chapter, we will explore strategies to detach yourself from the narcissistic influence and break free from their control. These strategies will empower you to regain your independence, reclaim your life, and build a healthier future. Let's delve into the following sections:

4.1 Understanding the Power of Detachment

- Recognizing the need for detachment to protect your emotional well-being.

- Letting go of the desire for validation and acceptance from the narcissist.

- Embracing the concept of emotional detachment as a healthy coping mechanism

4.2 Establishing No-Contact or Low-Contact

- Recognizing the benefits of limited or no contact with the narcissist

- Setting clear boundaries and minimizing communication to protect yourself.

- Strategies for implementing and maintaining no-contact or low-contact arrangements.

4.3 Healing and Self-Rebuilding

- Nurturing self-care practices to promote emotional healing and self-rebuilding.

- Engaging in activities that bring you joy, fulfillment, and personal growth.

- Seeking professional support and therapy to address the emotional wounds caused by the narcissistic relationship.

4.4 Building a Support Network

- Identifying and nurturing relationships with supportive individuals

- Seeking support from friends, family, or support groups who understand your experiences.

- Utilizing online resources and forums for connecting with others who have dealt with narcissistic abuse.

4.5 Reinventing Your Identity

- Rediscovering your authentic self and reclaiming your identity

- Exploring your passions, interests, and goals outside the narcissistic relationship

- Cultivating self-compassion and embracing your worth beyond the narcissist's perception

4.6 Strengthening Emotional Resilience

- Developing resilience to cope with triggers and setbacks.

- Practicing mindfulness, meditation, and stress-reduction techniques

- Building a toolbox of coping mechanisms to navigate future challenges.

4.7 Creating a New Narrative

- Shifting your perspective and reframing your experiences

- Focusing on personal growth, empowerment, and resilience

- Embracing a positive and optimistic outlook for your future

Breaking free from a narcissistic relationship is a courageous journey that requires strength, determination, and self-compassion. By implementing the strategies outlined in this chapter, you can liberate yourself from the narcissist's control, reclaim your autonomy, and embark on a path of healing and personal growth. Remember, you deserve a life filled with respect, love, and authentic connections.

4.1 The Art of Detachment: Emotionally Disengaging

Detaching yourself emotionally from a narcissistic individual is a crucial step towards breaking free from their toxic influence. It allows you to regain control over your emotions, protect your well-being, and create space for healing. In this section, we will explore the art of detachment and strategies for emotionally disengaging from a narcissist:

1. Recognize the Need for Detachment: Acknowledge that detaching from the narcissist is essential for your emotional well-being. Understand that their behavior is unlikely to change, and continuing to invest your emotions and energy in the relationship will only perpetuate the cycle of abuse. Embrace the idea that detaching does not mean indifference or lack of empathy but rather self-preservation.

2. Set Boundaries: Establish clear boundaries to protect yourself from further emotional harm. Define what behavior is acceptable and what is not. Communicate your boundaries assertively and consistently enforce them. This sends a message to the narcissist that you are no longer willing to

tolerate their manipulations and mistreatment.

3. Practice Emotional Awareness: Develop self-awareness and become attuned to your emotions in the presence of the narcissist. Recognize when you are being triggered, manipulated, or emotionally drained. By identifying your emotional responses, you can consciously choose not to engage and detach yourself from the situation.

4. Minimize Emotional Reactivity: Narcissists often provoke emotional reactions to maintain control and power over you. Practice emotional self-regulation by consciously choosing not to react impulsively to their provocations. Take deep breaths, count to ten, or remove yourself from the situation temporarily. Responding calmly and assertively instead of reacting emotionally reduces their influence over you.

5. Focus on Self-Care: Prioritize self-care as a means of nurturing yourself during the detachment process. Engage in activities that promote relaxation, self-reflection, and personal growth. Take care of your physical health, engage in hobbies you enjoy, and surround yourself with positive influences. Self-care strengthens your emotional resilience and reinforces your commitment to detaching from the narcissist.

6. Seek Support: Reach out to a therapist or support group specializing in narcissistic abuse. They can provide guidance, validation, and strategies for detachment. Connecting with others who have experienced similar situations can help you feel understood and supported throughout your journey.

7. Practice Acceptance: Accept that you cannot change the narcissist or their behavior. Release any unrealistic expectations of them becoming the person you desire them to be. Instead, focus on accepting the reality of the situation and directing your energy toward your own healing and growth.

8. Reframe Your Perspective: Shift your perspective by reframing your experiences with the narcissist. Recognize that their behavior is a reflection of their own insecurities and not a reflection of your worth or value as a person. Reframe the situation as an opportunity for personal growth and learning, allowing you to emerge stronger and more resilient.

Remember, detachment is a process that takes time and effort. Be patient with yourself as you navigate through the emotions and challenges that arise. By consciously practicing detachment, you create space for healing, reclaim your sense of self, and pave the way for a healthier and more fulfilling future.

4.2 No Contact Rule: Establishing Distance for Healing

Implementing the no-contact rule is a powerful strategy for breaking free from the influence of a narcissist and facilitating your healing process. This rule involves cutting off all communication and contact with the narcissist, allowing you to regain control over your life and prioritize your well-being. Here are some key aspects of implementing the no-contact rule:

1. Understand the Purpose: Recognize that the no-contact rule is not a punishment for the narcissist but a necessary step for your own healing. It creates a physical and emotional distance that protects you from further manipulation, gaslighting, and emotional harm. It allows you to focus on your own well-being and break the cycle of dependency.

2. Establish Clear Boundaries: Clearly communicate your decision to implement the no-contact rule to the narcissist, if appropriate and safe to do so. Clearly state your boundaries and intentions, emphasizing that you need time and space to heal. Be assertive and firm in your communication,

avoiding unnecessary explanations or justifications.

3. Block All Communication Channels: Block the narcissist's phone number, email address, and social media accounts to prevent any direct or indirect communication. Remove their presence from your online platforms and establish strict privacy settings. Consider changing your phone number or email address if necessary to ensure complete disconnection.

4. Inform Mutual Connections: Inform mutual friends, family members, or acquaintances about your decision to implement the no-contact rule. Request their understanding and support in maintaining your boundaries. Ask them to refrain from providing information about you to the narcissist and to respect your need for distance.

5. Create a Supportive Environment: Surround yourself with a strong support system of friends, family, or a support group who understand your situation. Share your experiences, feelings, and challenges with them. Seek their support, encouragement, and validation throughout the no-contact process. Having a supportive network can help you stay committed to your decision.

6. Establish Self-Care Practices: Focus on self-care activities that promote your well-being and aid in your healing process. Engage in activities that bring you joy, practice relaxation techniques, exercise regularly, maintain a healthy diet, and prioritize good sleep. Nurture your emotional, physical, and mental well-being during this time.

7. Redirect Your Energy: Redirect your energy and focus toward personal growth, hobbies, and goals. Invest your time and efforts in activities that empower you, build your self-esteem, and promote self-discovery. This redirection helps fill the void left by the absence of the narcissist and reinforces your sense of self outside of the toxic relationship.

8. Stay Committed to No Contact: Remind yourself of the reasons why you implemented the no contact rule whenever you experience doubts or temptations to reconnect. Stay committed to your decision, even if it feels challenging at times. Remember that breaking the no-contact rule often leads to further pain and setbacks in your healing journey.

9. Seek Professional Help if Needed: Consider seeking therapy or counseling to navigate the emotional challenges that arise during the no-contact period. A qualified professional can provide guidance, validation, and tools to

help you process your emotions, heal from the abuse, and develop healthy coping strategies.

Implementing the no-contact rule is a vital step in reclaiming your power and rebuilding your life after narcissistic abuse. It allows you to focus on your healing, rediscover your authentic self, and create a future free from the toxic influence of the narcissist. Stay strong, stay committed, and remember that you deserve a life filled with respect, love, and healthy connections.

4.3 Gray Rock Technique: Neutralizing Their Power

The Gray Rock technique is a powerful strategy for dealing with narcissists by minimizing their ability to manipulate and provoke emotional reactions. By adopting a neutral and unresponsive approach, you can effectively reduce their control over you and protect your emotional well-being. Here's how to utilize the Gray Rock technique:

1. Understand the Purpose: Recognize that the Gray Rock technique aims to make yourself uninteresting and emotionally unresponsive to the narcissist. The goal is to remove their source of narcissistic supply by not providing the reactions or attention they seek.

2. Limit Emotional Expression: Refrain from showing emotional reactions, whether positive or negative, in the presence of the narcissist. Avoid displaying strong emotions, such as anger, sadness, or excitement, as they can be used as tools for manipulation. Maintain a calm and neutral demeanor when interacting with them.

3. Keep Conversations Superficial: During conversations, focus on keeping the topics

light and impersonal. Share minimal personal information and avoid discussing your emotions, thoughts, or vulnerabilities. Steer the conversation towards neutral subjects like current events or general interests, deflecting any attempts to delve into personal matters.

4. Provide Minimal Feedback: Minimize the feedback you give to the narcissist. Keep your responses brief, factual, and devoid of emotional content. Avoid engaging in discussions or debates that can lead to emotional entanglement or manipulation. Provide neutral responses without revealing personal opinions or details.

5. Maintain Boundaries: Consistently enforce your boundaries and do not waver in your resolve. Clearly communicate your limits and expectations to the narcissist, making it clear that certain topics or behaviors are off-limits. Refuse to engage in activities or discussions that compromise your well-being or violate your boundaries.

6. Reduce Availability: Limit your availability to the narcissist by creating physical and emotional distance. Respond to their communications with a delay, giving the impression that you have a busy and fulfilling life outside of their influence. Avoid being readily accessible or at their beck and call.

7. Focus on Self-Care: Prioritize self-care practices to strengthen your emotional well-being. Engage in activities that bring you joy, relaxation, and fulfillment. Invest your time and energy in cultivating positive relationships, pursuing personal goals, and nourishing your physical and mental health.

8. Seek Support: Seek support from trusted friends, family members, or a support group who understands your experiences. Share your journey and experiences with them, receiving validation and encouragement. Surround yourself with individuals who provide a safe and supportive environment.

9. Practice Patience: Implementing the Gray Rock technique may take time and practice. Be patient with yourself as you learn to detach emotionally and neutralize the narcissist's power. It may be challenging at first, but with consistent effort, it becomes easier to maintain emotional distance.

Remember, the Gray Rock technique is an effective strategy for minimizing the narcissist's ability to manipulate and control you. By adopting a neutral and unresponsive stance, you regain power over your own emotions and protect yourself from their toxic influence. Stay committed to your well-being, prioritize self-care, and focus on building a fulfilling life beyond the narcissist's reach.

4.4 Support Systems: Building a Strong Network

Building a strong support system is essential for navigating the challenges of dealing with a narcissist. Surrounding yourself with understanding and empathetic individuals who can provide emotional support, guidance, and validation is crucial for your well-being. Here are some strategies for building a strong support system:

1. Identify Trustworthy Individuals: Identify people in your life whom you trust and feel safe confiding in. This can include close friends, family members, or even support groups for individuals who have experienced narcissistic abuse. Seek out those who have a genuine understanding of narcissism and its effects, as they are more likely to provide the support you need.

2. Communicate Your Needs: Articulate your needs to your support system. Let them know what kind of support you require, whether it's a listening ear, practical advice, or emotional validation. Clearly express your boundaries and how they can best support you during challenging times.

3. Seek Professional Help: Consider engaging the services of a therapist or counselor who specializes in narcissistic abuse. A trained professional can provide you with the tools and guidance to navigate the healing process effectively. They can help you process your emotions, develop coping strategies, and work through any trauma you may have experienced.

4. Join Support Groups: Consider joining support groups or online communities specifically tailored to individuals recovering from narcissistic abuse. These groups provide a safe space where you can share your experiences, receive validation, and connect with others who have gone through similar situations. Hearing others' stories can help you feel understood and less alone in your journey.

5. Educate Yourself: Educate yourself about narcissistic personality disorder, abuse dynamics, and recovery. Read books, articles, and reputable online resources to gain a deeper understanding of narcissism and its impact. This knowledge will empower you in conversations with your support system and help you make informed decisions about your healing process.

6. Practice Active Listening: Develop active listening skills when engaging with your

support system. Offer them the same level of empathy and understanding they provide you. Listening attentively and without judgment creates a nurturing environment for open communication and strengthens the bond between you and your support network.

7.   Nurture Reciprocal Relationships: Invest time and energy in building reciprocal relationships with your support system. Offer support and be there for them when they need it. Cultivate a balanced give-and-take dynamic where both parties feel valued and supported. Building these relationships fosters a sense of belonging and mutual support.

8.   Attend Workshops and Seminars: Explore workshops, seminars, or conferences focused on narcissistic abuse and recovery. These events provide opportunities to learn from experts, connect with survivors, and gain valuable insights and tools for healing. Participating in such events can be empowering and contribute to your overall growth and well-being.

9.   Prioritize Self-Care: Remember to prioritize self-care while navigating the challenges of dealing with a narcissist. Engage in activities that nourish your mind, body, and soul. Practice self-compassion, set boundaries,

and give yourself permission to heal and grow. By taking care of yourself, you'll be better equipped to handle the complexities of the healing process.

Building a strong support system is a vital component of your healing journey. Surrounding yourself with individuals who understand and support you will provide the encouragement and validation you need to overcome the challenges of dealing with a narcissist. Together, you can reclaim your power, heal from the abuse, and create a fulfilling and empowered life.

Chapter 5: Legal and Professional Considerations

Dealing with a narcissist often involves navigating complex legal and professional aspects to protect yourself and your interests. This chapter provides guidance on important considerations when dealing with a narcissist in these contexts. It covers:

5.1 Legal Options: Understanding Your Rights

- Familiarize yourself with the legal options available to you, such as obtaining a restraining order or seeking legal protection from harassment or abuse. Research the laws in your jurisdiction regarding domestic violence, harassment, and stalking, as they vary across different regions.

- Consult with a qualified attorney who specializes in family law or domestic abuse cases. They can provide you with personalized advice, help you understand your rights, and guide you through the legal processes.

- Document incidents of abuse or harassment by maintaining a detailed record of dates, times, locations, and descriptions of the incidents. Gather any evidence, such as text messages, emails, or photographs, that can support your case. This documentation can be valuable in legal proceedings.

- Consider gathering witnesses or testimonies from individuals who have witnessed the narcissist's abusive behavior. Their accounts can strengthen your case and provide additional support.

5.2 Professional Support: Seeking Therapeutic Assistance

- Engage in therapy or counseling to address the emotional and psychological effects of narcissistic abuse. A mental health professional can help you process your experiences, develop coping strategies, and rebuild your self-esteem.

- Choose a therapist who specializes in trauma, narcissistic abuse, or post-traumatic stress disorder (PTSD). They will have the expertise to guide you through the healing process and support your emotional well-being.

- Collaborate with your therapist to develop a safety plan to address any ongoing threats or risks posed by the narcissist. This plan may include strategies for maintaining physical and emotional safety, accessing emergency support, and managing potential triggers.

- Explore therapeutic modalities that are effective in treating trauma, such as cognitive-behavioral therapy (CBT), dialectical behavior therapy (DBT), or eye movement desensitization and reprocessing (EMDR). These approaches can assist in processing and healing the emotional wounds caused by narcissistic abuse.

5.3 Professional Reputation: Managing Your Image

- If the narcissist is present in your professional life, take steps to protect your reputation and minimize their potential impact on your career. Document instances of workplace harassment or sabotage, and report them to the appropriate authorities within your organization.

- Maintain a professional demeanor and focus on excelling in your work. Avoid engaging in gossip or negative discussions about the narcissist, as it may reflect poorly on your professionalism. Instead, seek support from trusted colleagues or mentors outside of your immediate work environment.

- Consider consulting with an employment attorney if you believe your professional rights or opportunities have been compromised due to the narcissist's actions. They can advise you on potential legal remedies or actions you can take to protect your career.

- Utilize professional networks and organizations for support and career advancement opportunities. Engaging with like-minded professionals can provide you with valuable connections, resources, and opportunities outside the toxic influence of the narcissist.

5.4 Financial Considerations: Protecting Your Assets

- If you share financial assets or have joint accounts with the narcissist, consult with a financial advisor or attorney to explore your options for separating your finances. They can guide you through the process of dividing assets, securing your financial independence, and protecting your financial future.

- Review and update legal documents, such as wills, trusts, or powers of attorney, to ensure they accurately reflect your wishes and exclude the narcissist from having control or access to your assets.

- Be vigilant about monitoring your financial accounts for any suspicious or unauthorized activity. If you suspect financial abuse or fraud by the narcissist, report it to the appropriate authorities and take steps to secure your financial information.

- Consider seeking professional advice on creating a budget, managing debt, and establishing financial independence. Developing financial literacy and stability will empower you to regain control over your financial well-being.

Navigating the legal and professional aspects of dealing with a narcissist can be challenging. By understanding your legal rights, seeking professional support, managing your professional reputation, and protecting your financial interests, you can mitigate the negative impact of the narcissist and prioritize your well-being and future success. Remember, consult with legal and professional experts who can provide personalized guidance based on your specific circumstances.

5.1 Seeking Professional Help: Therapy and Counseling Options

Dealing with a narcissist can have significant emotional and psychological effects. Seeking professional help through therapy and counseling is an essential step toward healing and reclaiming your life. Here are some therapy and counseling options to consider:

1. Individual Therapy: Individual therapy provides a safe and confidential space for you to work through the effects of narcissistic abuse. A qualified therapist can help you process your emotions, understand patterns of behavior, and develop coping strategies. Look for a therapist who specializes in trauma, abuse recovery, or narcissistic personality disorder.

2. Trauma Therapy: Narcissistic abuse often leaves deep emotional scars and can result in symptoms of trauma. Trauma-focused therapy, such as Eye Movement Desensitization and Reprocessing (EMDR), Cognitive Processing Therapy (CPT), or Somatic Experiencing, can help you process and heal from traumatic experiences.

3. Support Groups: Joining a support group specifically for survivors of narcissistic abuse can provide validation, understanding, and a sense of community. Hearing others' stories and sharing your own can be empowering and offer valuable insights. Look for local support groups or online communities that focus on narcissistic abuse recovery.

4. Couples or Family Therapy: If the narcissist is a partner, family member, or co-parent, couples or family therapy can be helpful in addressing communication issues, setting boundaries, and navigating complex dynamics. However, it's important to assess the safety and willingness of all parties involved before pursuing this option.

5. Online Counseling: Online counseling platforms offer convenience and accessibility, allowing you to connect with licensed therapists remotely. These platforms often provide a wide range of therapists specializing in various areas, including narcissistic abuse. Ensure that the platform you choose prioritizes client confidentiality and employs licensed professionals.

6. Evidenced-Based Therapies: Consider therapies with a strong evidence base, such as Cognitive-Behavioral Therapy (CBT), Dialectical Behavior Therapy (DBT), or Acceptance and Commitment Therapy (ACT).

These approaches focus on identifying negative thought patterns, developing healthy coping skills, and fostering resilience.

7. Holistic Approaches: Explore holistic therapies that complement traditional approaches, such as mindfulness, meditation, yoga, or art therapy. These practices can help you reconnect with yourself, reduce stress, and promote overall well-being.

8. Therapeutic Modalities: Research different therapeutic modalities to find an approach that resonates with you. Some options include psychodynamic therapy, schema therapy, narrative therapy, or solution-focused therapy. Each modality has its own focus and techniques, so finding the right fit is important for your healing journey.

Remember, finding the right therapist is essential for effective therapy. Take the time to research and interview potential therapists to ensure they have experience in working with survivors of narcissistic abuse. Trust your instincts and choose someone with whom you feel comfortable and supported.

Seeking professional help is a courageous step towards healing and reclaiming your life. Through therapy and counseling, you can gain insight, develop coping strategies, and rebuild your self-esteem and sense of self-worth. Remember, healing takes time,

and you deserve the support and guidance necessary
to navigate this journey successfully.

5.2 Documentation and Evidence: Protecting Yourself

When dealing with a narcissist, it is crucial to protect yourself by documenting incidents, gathering evidence, and maintaining a record of the abuse. Documentation and evidence can be valuable in legal proceedings, ensuring your safety, and validating your experiences. Here are some important considerations:

1. Detailed Incident Journal: Keep a detailed journal documenting incidents of narcissistic abuse. Include dates, times, locations, and descriptions of the abusive behavior. Be specific about what was said or done, how it made you feel, and any witnesses present. This journal can serve as a powerful record of the narcissist's patterns of behavior.

2. Preserve Correspondence: Save any emails, text messages, voicemails, or other written communication from the narcissist that demonstrate their abusive behavior or manipulation. Take screenshots or make copies of these correspondences and store them securely.

3. Maintain a Safety Log: If you feel threatened or fear for your safety, create a safety log.

Record any instances of stalking, harassment, or threats made by the narcissist. Include details such as dates, times, locations, and descriptions of the incidents. If there are witnesses, note their names and contact information.

4. Gather Witness Testimonies: If there are witnesses to the narcissist's abusive behavior, consider asking them to provide written or verbal testimonies documenting what they have observed. These testimonies can support your case and lend credibility to your experiences.

5. Seek Professional Documentation: Obtain professional documentation to support your claims of abuse. This may include medical records, therapy notes, or evaluations conducted by mental health professionals who have assessed the impact of the abuse on your well-being.

6. Preserve Physical Evidence: If there is physical evidence of abuse, such as damaged property or injuries, photograph or document it as soon as possible. Ensure that the evidence is preserved in a safe place, and consider making backup copies in case they are needed in the future.

7. Record Audio or Video: In some circumstances, it may be necessary to

discreetly record interactions with the narcissist to capture their abusive behavior or manipulation. However, be aware of the legal implications regarding recording without consent in your jurisdiction. Consult with a legal professional to understand the laws and regulations governing audio or video recordings.

8. Maintain Privacy and Security: Keep your documentation and evidence in a secure location, such as a password-protected digital folder or a locked physical storage space. If using digital methods, consider encrypting sensitive files. Protect your privacy by ensuring that only trusted individuals have access to this information.

9. Consult with Legal Professionals: If you are considering legal action or need guidance on how to protect yourself legally, consult with an attorney experienced in family law, domestic abuse, or harassment cases. They can provide personalized advice based on your situation and guide you through the legal processes.

Remember, documenting and gathering evidence is essential, but your safety and well-being should always be the priority. If you feel threatened or at immediate risk, contact local authorities or seek assistance from a trusted support network.

5.3 Legal Actions: Understanding Your Rights

When dealing with a narcissist, it is important to understand your legal rights and options. Taking appropriate legal actions can help protect yourself, establish boundaries, and seek justice. Here are some key considerations regarding legal actions:

1. Educate Yourself on the Law: Familiarize yourself with the laws and legal processes relevant to your situation. Research laws related to domestic violence, harassment, stalking, restraining orders, and any other applicable laws in your jurisdiction. Understanding your rights and the legal remedies available to you is crucial in making informed decisions.

2. Consult with an Attorney: Seek legal advice from an attorney who specializes in family law, domestic abuse, or harassment cases. They can provide personalized guidance based on your circumstances and help you understand the legal options available. An attorney can also assist you in navigating the legal system and represent your interests.

3. Obtain a Restraining Order or Protection Order: If you fear for your safety or are

experiencing harassment or threats from the narcissist, consider obtaining a restraining order or protection order. These legal orders prohibit the narcissist from contacting or approaching you, providing a legal framework to enforce boundaries and protect your well-being. Consult with your attorney to understand the process and requirements for obtaining such orders in your jurisdiction.

4. Gather Evidence: As mentioned in the previous section, documentation and evidence play a vital role in legal proceedings. Collect and organize any evidence, such as documentation of abuse, witness testimonies, photographs, or audio/video recordings that support your claims. Presenting compelling evidence can strengthen your case and support your legal actions.

5. Report Incidents: If you have been a victim of abuse, harassment, or any illegal activities by the narcissist, consider reporting these incidents to the appropriate authorities. This may include filing a police report or notifying relevant agencies, such as child protective services or workplace human resources. Reporting incidents can create an official record and initiate investigations if necessary.

6. Consider Legal Remedies: Depending on the specific circumstances, you may have legal remedies available to you. This can include pursuing a civil lawsuit for damages resulting from the narcissist's actions, seeking a modification of child custody or visitation arrangements, or addressing financial issues through legal channels. Consult with your attorney to explore the best course of action based on your situation.

7. Preserve Your Legal Rights: During legal proceedings, it is important to protect your legal rights. Follow your attorney's advice, provide accurate and thorough information, and maintain proper documentation of all legal interactions. Adhere to court orders, attend scheduled hearings, and comply with legal obligations to ensure your interests are safeguarded.

8. Maintain Privacy and Safety: When pursuing legal actions, consider the potential impact on your privacy and safety. Share sensitive information only with trusted individuals and take precautions to protect your personal information from the narcissist. If necessary, consult with your attorney to explore additional measures for your safety, such as requesting confidentiality orders or redacting sensitive information from court documents.

Remember, legal processes can be complex and vary depending on your jurisdiction. It is crucial to work closely with a qualified attorney who can guide you through the legal system and advocate for your rights. Prioritize your safety and well-being throughout the legal process, seeking support from professionals and support networks to navigate the challenges of dealing with a narcissist legally.

5.4 Co-parenting with a Narcissist: Strategies for Protecting Children

Co-parenting with a narcissist can be challenging, as their manipulative behaviors and self-centeredness can negatively impact children. It is important to prioritize the well-being and safety of your children while navigating the co-parenting relationship. Here are some strategies to consider:

1. Establish Clear Boundaries: Set clear and consistent boundaries with the narcissistic co-parent. Clearly communicate expectations regarding parenting responsibilities, schedules, and decision-making. Stick to the boundaries you've established and avoid engaging in power struggles or arguments.

2. Focus on the Best Interests of the Children: Keep the best interests of your children at the forefront of your decision-making. Make choices that prioritize their physical and emotional well-being, stability, and development. This may involve compromising on certain matters for the sake of creating a healthier co-parenting environment.

3. Maintain Communication Channels: Establish communication channels that minimize direct contact and potential conflicts. Consider using email or a co-parenting app to communicate important information about the children. Keep communication brief, focused on the children's needs, and avoid personal attacks or engaging in heated discussions.

4. Document Communication and Incidents: Maintain a record of all communication with the narcissistic co-parent. Keep copies of emails, text messages, or any other relevant documentation. This documentation can be useful in case of disputes or legal proceedings.

5. Parallel Parenting: In high-conflict situations, parallel parenting can be an effective approach. This involves disengaging from direct communication with the narcissistic co-parent and minimizing interaction. Each parent independently makes decisions and follows their own routines, reducing conflict and stress.

6. Seek Mediation or Parenting Coordination: If communication and cooperation are consistently challenging, consider involving a mediator or parenting coordinator. These professionals can help facilitate communication, guide decision-making, and

provide neutral perspectives. They can also assist in developing a detailed parenting plan that addresses specific concerns and reduces opportunities for conflict.

7. Shield Children from Conflict: Minimize exposure to conflict between you and the narcissistic co-parent. Refrain from speaking negatively about the co-parent in front of the children, as this can create emotional distress and loyalty conflicts. Create a safe and supportive environment for your children, and provide them with age-appropriate explanations regarding any changes or challenges they may experience.

8. Encourage Healthy Coping Mechanisms: Teach your children healthy coping mechanisms to navigate their relationship with the narcissistic co-parent. Help them develop skills to recognize manipulative behaviors, maintain their self-esteem, and establish boundaries. Encourage open communication and assure them that they can express their feelings without judgment.

9. Seek Professional Support for Children: If your children are struggling emotionally or displaying signs of distress, consider involving a qualified therapist or counselor. They can provide a safe space for your children to process their feelings, develop coping strategies, and build resilience.

10. Document Concerns for Legal Purposes: If the narcissistic co-parent's behavior raises serious concerns about the children's well-being, document specific incidents, behaviors, or patterns. This documentation may be useful in legal proceedings to demonstrate the need for protective measures or modifications to custody arrangements. Consult with your attorney to understand the legal implications and requirements.

Remember, protecting your children from the negative effects of co-parenting with a narcissist requires consistent effort, patience, and resilience. Focus on creating a supportive environment for your children, promoting their emotional well-being, and seeking professional guidance when necessary. By prioritizing their needs and providing a stable and loving environment, you can help them navigate the challenges posed by the narcissistic co-parent.

Chapter 6: Healing and Thriving: Rebuilding Your Life

Recovering from the impact of dealing with a narcissist requires time, self-care, and intentional efforts to rebuild your life. This chapter explores strategies and practices that can support your healing journey and help you thrive:

6.1 Understanding the Aftermath: Reflect on the emotional, psychological, and social impact of the narcissistic relationship. Acknowledge and validate your experiences, recognizing that healing is a gradual process. Understand that it is normal to have a range of emotions, including anger, sadness, and confusion, as you navigate the aftermath.

6.2 Practicing Self-Compassion: Be kind and gentle with yourself during the healing process. Practice self-compassion by acknowledging your pain, accepting your emotions, and treating yourself with understanding and patience. Cultivate self-care rituals that nourish your mind, body, and soul.

6.3 Seeking Therapy and Support: Consider engaging in therapy or counseling to address the emotional wounds caused by the narcissistic relationship. A trained professional can provide guidance, tools, and techniques to support your healing journey. Additionally, seek support from trusted friends, family members, or support groups who can provide validation, empathy, and a safe space for sharing your experiences.

6.4 Rebuilding Self-Esteem and Identity: Reconnect with your authentic self and rebuild your self-esteem. Engage in activities that bring you joy and a sense of accomplishment. Set realistic goals and celebrate your achievements, no matter how small. Surround yourself with positive influences that encourage your growth and self-acceptance.

6.5 Establishing Healthy Relationships: Learn from your experiences and develop healthier relationship patterns. Set clear boundaries, practice effective communication, and prioritize mutual respect and trust. Surround yourself with supportive and caring individuals who contribute positively to your life.

6.6 Embracing Personal Growth: View the healing journey as an opportunity for personal growth and transformation. Explore new hobbies, interests, or skills that enhance your sense of self and bring fulfillment. Invest in ongoing self-improvement, whether it's through learning, self-reflection, or personal development programs.

6.7 Redefining Success and Happiness: Challenge societal definitions of success and happiness. Focus on cultivating a life that aligns with your values, passions, and purpose. Set meaningful goals that bring you fulfillment, rather than seeking external validation or approval.

6.8 Practicing Forgiveness and Letting Go: Consider the practice of forgiveness as a means of freeing yourself from the emotional burden of the narcissistic relationship. This does not mean condoning or forgetting the abuse, but rather releasing the anger and resentment that may hold you back. Letting go of the past allows you to reclaim your power and move forward.

6.9 Building Resilience: Cultivate resilience by developing coping strategies and emotional strength. Engage in self-reflection, mindfulness, and self-care practices that promote emotional well-being. Surround yourself with a strong support system and seek professional help when needed.

6.10 Embracing a Positive Future: Focus on creating a positive and fulfilling future for yourself. Set goals, visualize your desired outcomes, and take small steps toward manifesting your dreams. Embrace new opportunities, challenge yourself, and believe in your ability to create a life that is free from the negative influence of the narcissist.

Remember, healing and rebuilding after dealing with a narcissist is a unique journey for each individual. Be patient with yourself, celebrate your progress, and seek support when needed. As you implement these strategies, you can reclaim your life, cultivate resilience, and move forward on a path of healing and thriving.

6.1 Post-Narcissistic Recovery: Understanding the Healing Process

Recovering from the impact of a narcissistic relationship is a complex and multifaceted process. It involves not only healing from the emotional wounds inflicted by the narcissist but also rebuilding your self-esteem, establishing healthy boundaries, and rediscovering your sense of self. This chapter explores the stages and dynamics of post-narcissistic recovery to help you understand and navigate the healing process:

6.1.1 Acknowledging the Abuse: The first step in post-narcissistic recovery is acknowledging and recognizing the abuse you experienced. It involves coming to terms with the reality of the narcissistic relationship, understanding the dynamics of manipulation, and accepting that the narcissist's behavior was not your fault.

6.1.2 Validating Your Emotions: Allow yourself to experience and validate a range of emotions. You may feel anger, sadness, confusion, shame, or even guilt. It is important to acknowledge these emotions without judgment and give yourself permission to grieve the loss of the relationship you thought you had.

6.1.3 Educating Yourself: Empower yourself by learning about narcissism, its effects on victims, and the recovery process. Educating yourself about narcissistic personality disorder, the traits and patterns of narcissists, and the impact of their behaviors can provide validation and help you make sense of your experiences.

6.1.4 Establishing No Contact or Minimal Contact: Creating physical and emotional distance from the narcissist is crucial for your healing. This may involve implementing a strict no contact rule, minimizing contact to only essential matters (such as co-parenting), or establishing strong boundaries to protect yourself from further manipulation and abuse.

6.1.5 Seeking Professional Help: Consider seeking therapy or counseling to facilitate your healing journey. A qualified therapist can provide a safe and supportive space to process your emotions, gain insight into the dynamics of the relationship, and develop coping strategies to navigate the challenges of recovery.

6.1.6 Healing Trauma and Rebuilding Trust: Narcissistic abuse can cause deep emotional wounds and damage your ability to trust others. Working with a therapist specializing in trauma can help you heal from the psychological and emotional impact of the abuse, rebuild your self-worth, and restore your capacity for healthy relationships.

6.1.7 Rebuilding Self-Esteem and Self-Identity: Focus on rebuilding your self-esteem and self-identity, which may have been eroded by the narcissist's manipulation. Engage in self-care practices, engage in activities that bring you joy and fulfillment, and challenge negative self-beliefs. Surround yourself with supportive and uplifting individuals who appreciate and value you.

6.1.8 Establishing Healthy Boundaries: Learning to set and enforce healthy boundaries is essential in post-narcissistic recovery. Identify your needs, communicate them assertively, and learn to say no without guilt. Prioritize self-care and protect your emotional well-being by being selective about the people you allow into your life.

6.1.9 Cultivating Self-Compassion and Forgiveness: Practice self-compassion by treating yourself with kindness, understanding, and forgiveness. Let go of self-blame and recognize that you deserve love, respect, and happiness. While forgiveness of the narcissist may not be necessary or possible, forgiving yourself for any perceived shortcomings can be a powerful step toward healing.

6.1.10 Rebuilding Trust in Relationships: As you heal, it is natural to be cautious about entering new relationships. Take the time to rebuild trust in yourself and others. Surround yourself with trustworthy and supportive individuals who demonstrate empathy, respect, and healthy relationship dynamics.

6.1.11 Embracing Growth and Personal Development: View your recovery as an opportunity for personal growth and transformation. Explore new interests, engage in activities that nourish your soul, and challenge yourself to step outside your comfort zone. Seek personal development resources, such as books, workshops, or online courses, to support your growth journey.

6.1.12 Connecting with Supportive Communities: Seek out support groups, online communities, or forums where you can connect with others who have experienced similar relationships. Sharing your story, receiving validation, and gaining insights from others can be immensely healing and reassuring.

Remember, healing from the impact of a narcissistic relationship takes time and patience. Be gentle with yourself, celebrate your progress, and seek professional help when needed. Each individual's healing journey is unique, but by understanding the dynamics of post-narcissistic recovery, you can navigate the process with greater awareness, resilience, and self-compassion.

6.2 Self-Reflection and Growth: Rediscovering Your Authentic Self

Recovering from the effects of a narcissistic relationship involves rediscovering and reconnecting with your authentic self. The narcissist may have undermined your sense of identity and self-worth, but through self-reflection and intentional growth, you can reclaim your true essence. This chapter explores strategies and practices to help you embark on a journey of self-discovery and personal growth:

6.2.1 Self-Reflection: Engage in self-reflection to gain a deeper understanding of who you are beyond the influence of the narcissist. Ask yourself meaningful questions about your values, passions, strengths, and aspirations. Explore your core beliefs and challenge any negative self-perceptions that may have been instilled by the narcissistic relationship.

6.2.2 Embracing Authenticity: Embrace your authentic self by honoring your true desires, interests, and preferences. Allow yourself to express your thoughts, emotions, and needs authentically, without fear of judgment or rejection. Cultivate self-acceptance and celebrate your uniqueness.

6.2.3 Identifying Your Values: Clarify your personal values and use them as a compass to guide your decisions and actions. Identify what is truly important to you and align your life choices with these values. Living in alignment with your values fosters a sense of purpose and fulfillment.

6.2.4 Setting Meaningful Goals: Set meaningful and achievable goals that reflect your authentic desires and aspirations. Whether they are related to career, relationships, personal growth, or hobbies, setting goals gives you a sense of direction and purpose. Break them down into smaller steps and celebrate each milestone along the way.

6.2.5 Exploring New Interests and Passions: Use this opportunity to explore new interests and passions. Engage in activities that ignite your curiosity and bring you joy. Take up a new hobby, learn a new skill, or delve into a subject that fascinates you. This process of exploration can help you discover hidden talents and cultivate a sense of fulfillment.

6.2.6 Cultivating Healthy Relationships: Surround yourself with people who appreciate and support your authentic self. Seek out relationships that are based on mutual respect, trust, and genuine connection. Surrounding yourself with positive influences will nurture your growth and help you build healthy, fulfilling relationships.

6.2.7 Practicing Self-Care: Prioritize self-care as a way to nurture and honor your authentic self. Engage in activities that promote your physical, mental, and emotional well-being. Practice self-compassion and treat yourself with kindness, recognizing that your needs and self-care are important.

6.2.8 Engaging in Personal Development: Invest in your personal growth by engaging in personal development practices. This may include reading self-help books, attending workshops or seminars, seeking guidance from mentors, or working with a life coach. These resources can provide valuable insights, tools, and techniques to support your journey of self-discovery.

6.2.9 Challenging Limiting Beliefs: Identify and challenge any limiting beliefs or negative self-talk that may have been reinforced by the narcissistic relationship. Replace them with empowering and affirming beliefs that support your self-worth and potential. Seek support from therapists, coaches, or support groups to help you navigate this process.

6.2.10 Practicing Mindfulness: Incorporate mindfulness into your daily life to cultivate self-awareness and a deeper connection with your authentic self. Practice being fully present in the present moment, observing your thoughts and emotions without judgment. Mindfulness can help you become more attuned to your inner wisdom and intuition.

6.2.11 Embracing Growth and Transformation: Embrace personal growth and transformation as an ongoing process. View challenges and setbacks as opportunities for learning and growth. Embrace change and be open to new experiences and perspectives. Allow yourself to evolve and grow into the best version of yourself.

By engaging in self-reflection, embracing authenticity, and investing in personal growth, you can rediscover your authentic self and cultivate a life that aligns with your true desires and values. Remember, this is a journey of self-discovery and growth, and each step you take brings you closer to reclaiming your power and living a fulfilling life.

6.3 Building Resilience: Bouncing Back Stronger

Recovering from a narcissistic relationship requires resilience – the ability to adapt, bounce back, and thrive despite the challenges you have faced. Building resilience is a transformative process that empowers you to not only overcome the effects of the narcissistic relationship but also grow stronger and more capable of navigating future adversities. This chapter explores strategies and practices to help you cultivate resilience and embrace your inner strength:

6.3.1 Understanding Resilience: Gain a clear understanding of what resilience means and how it applies to your healing journey. Recognize that resilience is not about being unaffected by challenges but rather about your ability to recover, learn, and grow from them. Embrace the belief that you have the inner resources to face and overcome adversity.

6.3.2 Developing a Growth Mindset: Adopt a growth mindset, which is the belief that your abilities and intelligence can be developed through effort, practice, and learning. Embrace challenges as opportunities for growth and see setbacks as temporary hurdles rather than permanent limitations. Cultivate a positive and optimistic outlook on your ability to learn and overcome obstacles.

6.3.3 Practicing Self-Compassion: Be kind and compassionate toward yourself throughout your healing journey. Treat yourself with the same kindness, understanding, and support you would offer to a close friend. Practice self-compassion by acknowledging your pain, validating your emotions, and offering yourself comfort and encouragement.

6.3.4 Building a Supportive Network: Surround yourself with a supportive network of friends, family, and professionals who can provide emotional support, guidance, and encouragement. Seek out individuals who genuinely care about your well-being and who can help you navigate the challenges you may encounter on your path to healing.

6.3.5 Cultivating Emotional Intelligence: Develop emotional intelligence by enhancing your awareness and understanding of your own emotions and those of others. Practice managing and expressing your emotions in healthy ways, fostering empathy and compassion, and developing effective communication skills. Emotional intelligence equips you with the tools to navigate interpersonal relationships with resilience and empathy.

6.3.6 Developing Coping Strategies: Explore and develop healthy coping strategies that work for you. These may include practicing mindfulness, engaging in physical exercise, journaling, seeking therapy, or participating in creative outlets such as art, music, or writing. Experiment with different techniques to find what helps you regulate your emotions and maintain a sense of balance.

6.3.7 Embracing Change and Flexibility: Develop a mindset of adaptability and flexibility. Life is filled with unexpected twists and turns, and being able to adapt to change is a crucial aspect of resilience. Embrace new opportunities, be open to different perspectives, and cultivate a sense of curiosity and willingness to learn and grow.

6.3.8 Finding Meaning and Purpose: Seek meaning and purpose in your life. Reflect on your values, passions, and what truly matters to you. Identify activities, causes, or goals that give you a sense of purpose and contribute to your overall well-being. Align your actions with your values and pursue activities that bring meaning and fulfillment to your life.

6.3.9 Learning from Adversity: View adversity as an opportunity for growth and learning. Reflect on the lessons you have learned from your experiences with the narcissistic relationship. Identify the strengths and qualities that have emerged or been strengthened through the challenges you have faced. Allow these experiences to shape you into a wiser, more resilient individual.

6.3.10 Cultivating Gratitude: Practice gratitude by regularly acknowledging and appreciating the positive aspects of your life. Focus on the blessings, small joys, and moments of beauty. Cultivating gratitude shifts your perspective and helps you maintain a positive outlook even during difficult times.

6.3.11 Embracing Self-Empowerment: Reclaim your power and embrace self-empowerment. Recognize that you have control over your own thoughts, actions, and choices. Set meaningful goals, take proactive steps toward your healing, and celebrate your progress along the way. Trust in your own strength and resilience to create a life that is aligned with your values and aspirations.

By building resilience, you can transform your experiences with narcissism into a catalyst for growth and empowerment. Remember that resilience is not a fixed trait but a skill that can be developed and strengthened over time. Embrace the journey of building resilience, and you will emerge stronger, more confident, and better equipped to navigate the challenges and opportunities that life presents.

6.4 Cultivating Healthy Relationships: Redefining Trust and Intimacy

Recovering from a narcissistic relationship involves not only healing from the past but also cultivating healthy relationships in the future. Building trust and experiencing genuine intimacy may have been challenging in the aftermath of the narcissistic relationship, but it is possible to redefine these aspects of relationships. This chapter explores strategies and practices to help you cultivate healthy relationships based on trust, authenticity, and true intimacy:

6.4.1 Reflecting on Relationship Patterns: Take time to reflect on the patterns and dynamics of your past relationships, particularly the narcissistic ones. Identify the red flags, power imbalances, and unhealthy patterns that were present. This reflection will help you gain insight into what you want and need in a healthy relationship.

6.4.2 Setting Boundaries: Establish clear and healthy boundaries in your relationships. Learn to recognize and assert your needs and preferences, and communicate them to others. Boundaries create a sense of safety and protect your well-being, allowing you to maintain healthy dynamics with others.

6.4.3 Building Trust Gradually: Rebuilding trust after experiencing betrayal or manipulation can be challenging. Take the time to build trust gradually in new relationships. Allow trust to develop naturally as you observe consistent behaviors and experiences that demonstrate honesty, reliability, and respect.

6.4.4 Practicing Effective Communication: Develop effective communication skills to express yourself authentically and listen actively. Practice open and honest communication, expressing your thoughts, feelings, and needs clearly and respectfully. Encourage open dialogue in your relationships to foster understanding and connection.

6.4.5 Embracing Vulnerability: Embrace vulnerability as an essential component of genuine intimacy. Allow yourself to be open and authentic with others, sharing your thoughts, feelings, and fears. Recognize that vulnerability is a strength that deepens connections and fosters emotional intimacy.

6.4.6 Nurturing Emotional Safety: Prioritize emotional safety in your relationships. Create an environment where you and your partner or friends feel safe to express yourselves without judgment or fear of retaliation. Foster trust and support by practicing empathy, active listening, and validation.

6.4.7 Developing Healthy Conflict Resolution Skills: Learn and practice healthy conflict resolution skills to navigate disagreements in a constructive manner. Focus on active listening, empathy, and finding mutually beneficial solutions. Avoid engaging in power struggles or resorting to manipulative tactics.

6.4.8 Building a Supportive Network: Surround yourself with a supportive network of individuals who uplift and encourage you. Cultivate friendships and relationships with people who value and respect your boundaries, support your growth, and celebrate your successes.

6.4.9 Prioritizing Self-Care in Relationships: Continue prioritizing self-care within your relationships. Maintain your own individuality, interests, and personal growth while also nurturing the connection with your partner or friends. Remember that healthy relationships support and enhance your well-being, rather than depleting it.

6.4.10 Seeking Professional Support: If you find it challenging to navigate relationships or struggle with trust and intimacy issues, consider seeking professional support. A therapist or counselor can provide guidance, tools, and strategies to help you overcome obstacles and develop healthy relationship patterns.

Remember that cultivating healthy relationships takes time and self-awareness. Be patient with yourself and the process. Trust your intuition, set boundaries, and surround yourself with people who respect and value you. By redefining trust and intimacy, you can create meaningful connections built on mutual respect, authenticity, and love.

Conclusion: Your Journey to Freedom and Empowerment

Congratulations on embarking on your journey to deal with a narcissist and regain control of your life. Throughout this book, we have explored the complexities of narcissism, identified the traits and patterns of narcissistic behavior, and provided you with valuable strategies and tools to navigate the effects of narcissism on your emotional well-being.

Understanding narcissism and its impact is the first step toward breaking free from its grip. By recognizing the red flags and warning signs of narcissistic behavior, you have gained valuable insights into the manipulative tactics and cycles that narcissists employ. Armed with this knowledge, you can now take proactive steps to protect yourself and establish healthy boundaries.

Emotional abuse, gaslighting, and constant tension may have left you feeling drained and disconnected from your authentic self. However, through self-reflection, building resilience, and practicing self-care, you can rebuild your self-esteem and nurture your emotional well-being. Remember, you deserve love, respect, and happiness.

Detaching from the narcissist is a vital part of your journey toward freedom. By implementing strategies such as the No Contact Rule and the Gray Rock Technique, you can reclaim your power and create space for healing. Surrounding yourself with a supportive network and seeking professional help will further assist you in your recovery process.

As you heal, it is essential to consider the legal and professional aspects of dealing with a narcissist. Documenting evidence and understanding your rights can help protect you in legal situations. Additionally, co-parenting with a narcissist requires special strategies to safeguard the well-being of your children.

Rebuilding your life after narcissistic abuse is a transformative process. It begins with reconnecting with your authentic self, rediscovering your passions and values, and cultivating healthy relationships based on trust, communication, and mutual respect. By cultivating resilience, embracing self-empowerment, and fostering personal growth, you can create a life that is free from the toxic influence of narcissism.

Remember, your journey to freedom and empowerment is unique to you. Take the time to prioritize self-care, be patient with yourself, and celebrate your progress along the way. You are resilient, courageous, and capable of creating the life you deserve.

May this book serve as a guiding light on your path to healing, liberation, and thriving. Embrace your newfound knowledge and empower yourself to build a future filled with authenticity, joy, and genuine connections. You are not defined by the narcissist's actions, but rather by your resilience and ability to rise above. Embrace your journey to freedom and empowerment, and may it lead you to a life of happiness and fulfillment.

Appendix: Resources and Support Networks

Recovering from a narcissistic relationship can be a challenging and complex process. It is crucial to seek support and access resources that can provide guidance, validation, and additional tools to aid in your healing journey. This appendix offers a list of resources and support networks that you may find beneficial:

1. Therapists and Counselors: Professional therapy or counseling can provide a safe space for you to process your experiences, gain insights, and develop coping strategies. Seek licensed therapists experienced in trauma, abuse, or narcissistic personality disorder.

2. Support Groups: Joining support groups can offer a sense of community and understanding as you connect with others who have gone through similar experiences. They provide a platform to share stories, exchange advice, and receive support. Look for local support groups or online communities dedicated to healing from narcissistic abuse.

3. Books and Literature:

- "Psychopath Free: Recovering from Emotionally Abusive Relationships With Narcissists, Sociopaths, and Other Toxic People" by Jackson MacKenzie

- "The Narcissist's Playbook: How to Identify, Disarm, and Protect Yourself from Narcissists" by Dana Morningstar

- "Becoming the Narcissist's Nightmare: How to Devalue and Discard the Narcissist While Supplying Yourself" by Shahida Arabi

- "The Covert Passive-Aggressive Narcissist: Recognizing the Traits and Finding Healing After Hidden Emotional and Psychological Abuse" by Debbie Mirza

4. Online Resources:

- The National Domestic Violence Hotline (www.thehotline.org) provides resources, support, and a 24/7 helpline for those affected by abuse.

- Out of the Fog (www.outofthefog.net) offers

information, resources, and a supportive community for individuals dealing with personality disorders, including narcissism.

- The Mighty (www.themighty.com) features articles, personal stories, and a community that addresses mental health and personal growth topics, including narcissistic abuse.

5. Legal Support: If legal actions are necessary, consult with an attorney who specializes in family law or domestic abuse. They can guide you through the legal processes, provide advice on protecting your rights, and help you navigate any custody or divorce proceedings.

6. Self-Care Practices: Explore self-care practices that resonate with you. This may include mindfulness and meditation, physical exercise, journaling, creative outlets, nature walks, or engaging in activities that bring you joy and relaxation. Prioritize self-care as an integral part of your healing process.

Remember that everyone's healing journey is unique, and it's important to find the resources and support that best align with your needs and preferences. Be patient with yourself, and reach out for help when needed. You are not alone, and with the right support, you can heal, rebuild, and create a life free from the impact of narcissistic abuse.

Special Thanks

I would like to express my gratitude to everyone who contributed to the creation of this book on dealing with a narcissist. Writing a comprehensive guide on such a complex topic would not have been possible without the collective effort and expertise of various individuals and resources.

I would like to extend a special thanks to:

- Mental health professionals: Your dedication to understanding and treating narcissistic personality disorder has provided valuable insights and perspectives for this book. Your expertise has helped shed light on the intricacies of narcissism and its impact on individuals.

- Researchers and authors: The wealth of knowledge and research on narcissism has been instrumental in shaping the content of this book. Your contributions to the field have paved the way for a deeper understanding of this personality disorder.

- Survivors and individuals who have shared their stories: Your courage and willingness to share your personal experiences have been a driving force behind this book. Your stories have helped validate the struggles faced by those dealing with narcissists and have offered hope and inspiration to others on their healing journeys.

- Support networks and online communities: Your dedication to providing a safe and supportive space for survivors of narcissistic abuse is commendable. Your resources, discussions, and encouragement have played a significant role in helping individuals navigate their way through the challenges of dealing with narcissists.

- Editors and proofreaders: Your keen eye for detail and commitment to ensuring the accuracy and clarity of the content is deeply appreciated. Your expertise in refining the manuscript has contributed to the overall quality of this book.

- Friends and family: Your unwavering support, encouragement, and understanding throughout the writing process have been invaluable. Your belief in the importance of this topic and your continuous encouragement have kept me motivated and inspired.

Finally, I would like to express my heartfelt appreciation to the readers of this book. Your interest in understanding and dealing with narcissism is a testament to your resilience and commitment to personal growth. It is my hope that this book provides you with the knowledge, strategies, and support you need to navigate the complexities of dealing with a narcissist and embark on a journey toward healing, empowerment, and a brighter future.

Thank you all for your contributions and for joining me in this important endeavor.

Made in the USA
Monee, IL
30 January 2024

52553232R00072